Classic Recipes of
THAILAND

Classic Recipes of THAILAND

TRADITIONAL FOOD AND COOKING
IN 25 AUTHENTIC DISHES

JUDY BASTYRA AND BECKY JOHNSON

LORENZ BOOKS

This edition is published by Lorenz Books,
an imprint of Anness Publishing Ltd,
108 Great Russell Street,
London WC1B 3NA
info@anness.com
www.annesspublishing.com
twitter: @Anness_Books

If you like the images in this book and
would like to investigate using them for
publishing, promotions or advertising,
please visit our website
www.practicalpictures.com for more
information.

Publisher: Joanna Lorenz
Editor: Helen Sudell
Designer: Nigel Partridge
Recipe Photography: Nicki Dowey
Food Stylist: Lucy McKelvie
Stylist: Helen Trent
Production Controller: Pirong Wang

A CIP catalogue record for this book is
available from the British Library

PUBLISHER'S NOTE

Although the advice and information in this
book are believed to be accurate and true
at the time of going to press, neither the
authors nor the publisher can accept any
legal responsibility or liability for any errors
or omissions that may have been made nor
for any inaccuracies nor for any loss, harm
or injury that comes about from following
instructions or advice in this book.

PUBLISHER'S ACKNOWLEDGMENTS

The Publisher would like to thank the
following agencies for the use of their
images. Istock p6, 8, 6 (both), 10 , 12
(bottom left), 13.

Previously published as part of a larger
volume *Thai Food and Cooking*.

COOK'S NOTES

Bracketed terms are intended for American
readers. For all recipes, quantities are given
in both metric and imperial measures and,
where appropriate, in standard cups and
spoons. Follow one set of measures, but
not a mixture, because they are not
interchangeable.

Standard spoon and cup measures are
level. 1 tsp = 5ml, 1 tbsp = 15ml, 1 cup =
250ml/8fl oz. Australian standard
tablespoons are 20ml. Australian readers
should use 3 tsp in place of 1 tbsp for
measuring small quantities.

American pints are 16fl oz/2 cups.
American readers should use 20fl oz/2.5
cups in place of 1 pint when measuring
liquids.

Electric oven temperatures in this book are
for conventional ovens. When using a fan
oven, the temperature will probably need to
be reduced by about 10–20°C/20–40°F.
Since ovens vary, you should check with
your manufacturer's instruction book for
guidance.

The nutritional analysis given for each
recipe is calculated per portion (i.e. serving
or item), unless otherwise stated. If the
recipe gives a range, such as Serves 4–6,
then the nutritional analysis will be for the
smaller portion size, i.e. 6 servings. The
analysis does not include optional
ingredients, such as salt added to taste.

Medium (US large) eggs are used unless
otherwise stated.

Contents

Introduction

Thai cooks pride themselves on preparing simple, fresh dishes of excellent quality. Succulent fish from the sea, rice from the fields, aromatic herbs and spices, and locally grown fruits and vegetables are just a few of the delicious ingredients that are enjoyed throughout Thailand. Each region has its own specialities based on locally grown and harvested produce but there are common flavourings and culinary techniques that are used throughout the country, creating a wonderfully vibrant and varied cuisine.

Left: Terraced rice fields to the north of the city of Chiang Mai.

Eating Thai-style

For the Thai people, eating is always a pleasure and is an important feature of everyday life. At home, meals are shared and are based on *khao* (rice). The thai word 'to eat' is actually *kin khao* (to eat rice). A bowl of rice is usually placed at the centre of the table surrounded by condiments and other dishes. It is considered polite to begin the meal with a single spoonful of rice, symbolizing the importance of the grain within the Thai culture and way of life

The influence of the Buddhist tradition can be see in the Thai

Below: Rice is eaten at every meal in Thailand.

Above: A street vendor making crispy pancakes filled with cream and coconut.

approach to meat. Thais do not believe that meat should be eaten in large portions. It is served in small amounts, usually cut into pieces or shredded.

Traditional meals

The main Thai meal is usually the last one of the day. It will include a variety of dishes, which are served as soon as they are cooked. Steamed rice is served with a clear soup, a steamed dish, a fried dish, a salad and a spicy sauce, such as *kruang jim*, *nam pla* or *nam prik*. Once the main course has been cleared,

fresh fruit and a dessert are eaten. Desserts are mainly based on fruit or coconut, and rice or flour, and are often very sweet with a delicate, scented flavour.

Snack foods

Thais are keen snackers, and tasty morsels can be found on virtually every street. Freshly fried fruit is a popular snack that can be bought coated in sugar, salt or dried crushed chilli flakes. *Khao poot* (corn) is a common snack, either steamed and dunked in salty water or cooked over a brazier. *Salapoa*, which are steamed rice flour dumplings stuffed with pork or bean paste, are also very popular.

Another quick bite is *bah jang*, a delicious mixture of sticky rice and peanuts combined with pork, mushrooms, Chinese sausage or salty eggs. The mixture is wrapped in banana leaves, tied together with straw string, and hung in rows from vendor's carts.

Right: Steamed dumplings are a much-loved street snack.

Thai Festivals

The multitude of festivals and events that fill the Thai calendar are varied in origins. Some are religious (Theravada Buddhism is the prevalent religion), others celebrate the annual rice-farming cycle or express gratitude for produce for the land. Food plays an important part with large meals serving traditional and beautifully displayed food. Hawkers selling delicious meals and snacks also always appear at these large gatherings.

New Year Celebrations

Thai New Year's Day is 13 April but the festival is celebrated over three days. People make pilgrimages and practise merit-making, where food is offered to Buddhist monks (monks are only allowed to receive food as gifts). Water is an important feature of this celebration, symbolizing cleansing and renewal.

Festival of Light

The *Loy Krathong* ceremony, better knowm as the Festival of Light, takes place on the eve of the full moon in November. The festival begins when the full moon is in the sky. People carry *krathongs* – small lotus-shaped banana leaf boats containing candles, incense and coins – to nearby waterways. After lighting the candles and incense and saying a blessing, the *krathong* is set afloat for the spirits and Goddess of the Water. Across the country, the waterways are illuminated by thousands of tiny *krathongs* as they float off, carrying misfortune away from the owner into the darkness of the water.

Above: Lit krathongs float downstream in celebration of the Goddess of the Water.

Bun Bung Fai

Before the monsoons, around the second week of May, the skies of the north-eastern regions of Thailand are ablaze with the light and explosions from thousands of fireworks. This rocket festival marks the beginning of the rice-planting and ploughing season. The rockets are released to encourage a plentiful rainfall and a good harvest.

Rice Ploughing Ceremony

At around the same time as Bun Bung Fai, there is a rice-ploughing ceremony in Sanam Luang, Bangkok. It is an ancient Brahmin ceremony that aims to bless the farmers with bumper crops in the coming year. At a certain point in the ceremony, *Phraya Rake Na* – the Farming Lord – will plough an area of land near the palace to mark the start of the season. The cows are offered an assortment of different foods including grass, rice, corn, beans, liquor and water. The foods that the cows choose are used to predict the success of the harvest in the coming year.

The Sart Festival

This event, which marks the beginning of the rice-harvesting season, was originally a Brahmin festival celebrated in India at the end of the tenth lunar month. It is celebrated in Thailand in the Buddhist temple, but, in Thailand, the tenth lunar month is not the normal harvest time, so farmers plant a special type of flat rice, *khow mow*, that can be harvested at this time of year. *Khow mow* is used to prepare *krayasart*, which is a sweet confection made from rice and peanuts that is usually eaten with small bananas. *Krayasart* are offered to monks through merit-making before others enjoy them.

Regional Food Fairs

In December, Chiang Mai hosts many food and agriculture festivals and fairs. Between 8

Above: A traditional fruit carving at the Chiang Mai food festival.

and 12 December is the Chiang Mai Food Festival, which celebrates the art of Thai cuisine. Among many things, it features fruit and ice carving, demonstrations of food preparation and dessert-making. Over one hundred local food businesses set up stalls under the night sky. Mouthwatering cakes and confectionery sit side-by-side with classic local dishes such as *phat thai* and the spicy salad, *som tam*.

Below: A Buddhist monk receives gifts of food.

Thai Cuisine

Founded on simple ingredients of excellent quality, the Thai cuisine relies on five primary flavours that are used in differing proportions to produce a wonderful range of dishes. The five key flavours are salty, sweet, sour, bitter and hot. The secret to all Thai food lies in the subtle differences in the proportions of ingredients used, which can add layers of flavour and aroma. The cooking of each region, while using these basic flavours, has its own characteristics and produces an interesting array of local specialities.

Below: Shrimp paste will add salt to the meal.

Salty

This flavour enhances and brings out the tastes of other ingredients. It is usually added via salty ingredients rather than table salt. One of the most widely used of these is *nam pla*, which is a sauce made from fermented fish, while *kapi*, a salty shrimp paste, is used to add its own distinctive flavour to dishes. Other salty condiments include Thai oyster sauce (milder and more 'oystery' than its Chinese counterpart); light soy sauce; dark or light yellow bean sauce; dried fish or shrimp (which can be ground and added to soups or salads); salted plums; and salted preserved vegetables, such as cabbage or *mooli* (daikon).

Sweet

Thai food often has a subtle sweetness. Sweet ingredients such as palm sugar and coconut sugar are often added to savoury dishes to enhance the flavours of spices and herbs. Other sweetening agents include sweet black soy sauce, which is made by fermenting soy sauce with treacle (molasses); sweet pickled garlic; and brown rice syrup. Honey is also used as a sweetener.

Sour

Lime juice is one of the most popular sour flavourings because it not only adds a sour taste but helps to accentuate other flavours. Sour tamarind, often sold as wet tamarind, is also used as a souring agent. Both ingredients have a tenderizing effect on meats and fish. Various vinegars such as coconut, white distilled or the less sharp rice vinegar are also employed.

Bitter

The bitter flavour of Thai dishes is produced by ingredients such as herbs or dark green vegetables. These are generally one of the main ingredients of the recipe, so the bitterness must be balanced by adjusting the other four primary flavours.

Right: Fresh limes on sale at a market in Bangkok.

Above: Chinese chives have a strong pungent garlic flavour.

Hot

Despite the fiery reputation of the Thai cuisine, not all dishes are overpoweringly hot. However, Thais do have a great tolerance to spicy dishes, acquired from a lifetime's experience. The main source of heat is the chilli, which is sold fresh, dried or in pastes and sauces (*priks*). Before the chilli was introduced to thailand, heat was obtained from peppercorn, which are still used. Heat can also be introduced through ginger, onions and garlic. Chilli-based condiments such as crushed dried chillies and chilli paste are usually placed on the table so that diners can season the dish further, adding heat according to their own taste.

The Northern Cuisine

Unlike the rest of Thailand, where jasmine rice is favoured, northerners prefer sticky glutinous rice, which can be rolled into balls and dipped into sauces or curries. The curries are often thin because coconut milk, which is used as a thickener elsewhere, is not readily available. The dishes also tend to be less spicy than in other regions. Unusual ingredients found in the north include buffalo meat and giant beetles.

Food in the North East

North-eastern Thais have a reputation for adventurous eating. Some of the more unusual delicacies include ant eggs, grubworms, snail curry, grasshoppers and pungent fermented fish.

Cooking in the north east is usually very hot and spicy, using more chilli than is favoured in

Above: Rice is the most important ingredient for Thais.

other regions. The cuisine also shows a strong Laotian influence. A classic delicacy from Laos, which is served at celebrations, is *Khano buang* – crispy pancakes stuffed with dried shrimp and beansprouts.

Food in the Central Region

The traditional food of central Thailand is often plainer than that eaten elsewhere. A typical dish will consist of rice with stir-fried vegetables, fish from a nearby river, canal or paddy field, and a salad made from salted eggs, chillies, spring onion (scallion) and lime juice.

In the bustling hub of Bangkog, however, you can experience not only Thailand's regional cuisines, but also many international dishes. The city is a paradise for food lovers. Everywhere there is food on display and there are very many cafés and restaurants, as well as the street or river vendors.

Southern Cooking

Fish and shellfish are abundant in the south, which is almost completely surrounded by coastline. Many dishes feature rock lobsters, crabs, mussels, squid, prawns (shrimp) and scallops. They may be used in

Below: Prawns are often added to seafood dishes.

soup, grilled (broiled), steamed, or added to a curry.

Many different cultures and countries have influenced the cuisine of this region, and there is a strong Muslim presence, which can be seen in the food. Mussaman-style curry shows an Indian influence, while satay originates from Indonesia. The dishes of Songkhla and the island of Phuket, where the population is largely Chinese, show a definite Chinese influence.

Coconuts grow plentifully everywhere, providing milk for thickening soups and curries, and oil for frying. Fresh coconut is used in savoury and sweet dishes. Cashew nuts and pineapples also grow here. In general, the food is chilli-hot.

The Royal Palace Tradition

The tradition of food decoration and presentation originates from the court of the Grand Palace in Bangkok. Living within the walls of the inner palace was a large community of women who were trained in the running of an

Above: Coconut is used in many Thai meals.

elegant household. An integral part of their training was learning to prepare food. Importance was laid equally between flavour and aesthetic appeal.

One of the most visually impressive skills was that of vegetable and fruit carving, which was seen as a symbol of good food throughout Thailand. Huge watermelons and tiny chillies were turned into elaborate blossoming flowers, and pumpkins and ginger roots were cut into complicated abstract designs. These skills are still very much in evidence today in one variation or another on the Thai dining table.

Taste of Thailand

Taking pleasure in the preparation, cooking and presentation of food is central to the Thai culture and cuisine. Every dish is a delight to the senses and featured here are many classic meals from across the region. Snack on delicious Corn Fritters or deep-fried Tung Tong; cook up a traditional curry of Green Beef with Thai Aubergines, or Chicken and Lemon Grass; and indulge your sweet tooth with a portion of Fried Bananas wrapped in banana leaves. This selection of quintessential recipes will ensure you experience the very best of Thai food and cooking.

Left: Tasty snacks, crispy-fried rice cakes and hot dipping sauces are eaten daily across Thailand.

Omelette Soup

Serves 4

1 egg
15ml/1 tbsp groundnut (peanut) oil
900ml/1½ pints/3¾ cups
    vegetable stock
2 large carrots, finely diced
4 outer leaves Savoy
    cabbage, shredded
30ml/2 tbsp soy sauce
2.5ml/½ tsp granulated sugar
2.5ml/½ tsp ground black pepper
fresh coriander (cilantro) leaves,
    to garnish

VARIATION
Use pak choi (bok choy) instead of Savoy cabbage. In Thailand there are about forty different types of pak choi, including some miniature versions.

A very satisfying soup that is quick and easy to prepare. It is versatile, too, in that you can vary the vegetables according to what is available.

1 Put the egg in a bowl and beat lightly with a fork. Heat the oil in a small frying pan until it is hot, but not smoking. Pour in the egg and swirl the pan so that it coats the base evenly. Cook over a medium heat until the omelette has set and the underside is golden. Slide it out of the pan and roll it up like a pancake. Slice into 5mm/¼in rounds and set aside for the garnish.

2 Put the stock into a large pan. Add the carrots and cabbage and bring to the boil. Reduce the heat and simmer for 5 minutes, then add the soy sauce, granulated sugar and pepper.

3 Stir well, then pour into warmed bowls. Lay a few omelette rounds on the surface of each portion and complete the garnish with the coriander leaves.

Hot and Sweet Vegetable and Tofu Soup

Serves 4

1.2 litres/2 pints/5 cups vegetable
  stock
5–10ml/1–2 tsp Thai red curry paste
2 kaffir lime leaves, torn
40g/1½oz/3 tbsp palm sugar or light
  muscovado (brown) sugar
30ml/2 tbsp soy sauce
juice of 1 lime
1 carrot, cut into thin batons
50g/2oz baby spinach leaves, any
  coarse stalks removed
225g/8oz block silken tofu, diced

An interesting combination of hot, sweet and sour flavours that makes for a soothing, nutritious soup. It takes only minutes to make as the spinach and silken tofu are simply placed in bowls and covered with the flavoured hot stock.

1 Heat the stock in a large pan, then add the red curry paste. Stir constantly over a medium heat until the paste has dissolved. Add the lime leaves, sugar and soy sauce and bring to the boil.

2 Add the lime juice and carrot to the pan. Reduce the heat and simmer for 5–10 minutes. Place the spinach and tofu in four individual serving bowls and pour the hot stock on top to serve.

Chiang Mai Noodle Soup

1 Pour about one-third of the coconut milk into a large, heavy pan or wok. Bring to the boil over a medium heat, stirring frequently with a wooden spoon until the milk separates.

2 Add the curry paste and ground turmeric, stir to mix completely and cook until the mixture is fragrant.

3 Add the chunks of chicken and toss over the heat for about 2 minutes, making sure that all the chunks are thoroughly coated with the paste.

4 Add the remaining coconut milk, the chicken stock, fish sauce and soy sauce. Season with salt and pepper to taste. Bring to simmering point, stirring frequently, then lower the heat and cook gently for 7–10 minutes. Remove from the heat and stir in lime juice to taste.

5 Reheat the fresh egg noodles in boiling water, drain and divide among four to six warmed bowls. Divide the chunks of chicken among the bowls and ladle in the hot soup.

6 Top each serving with spring onions, chillies, shallots, pickled mustard leaves, fried garlic, coriander leaves and a fried noodle nest, if using. Serve immediately.

Serves 4–6

600ml/1 pint/2½ cups coconut milk
30ml/2 tbsp Thai red curry paste
5ml/1 tsp ground turmeric
450g/1lb chicken thighs, boned and
    cut into bitesize chunks
600ml/1 pint/2½ cups chicken stock
60ml/4 tbsp Thai fish sauce
15ml/1 tbsp dark soy sauce
juice of ½–1 lime
450g/1lb fresh egg noodles,
    blanched briefly in boiling water
salt and ground black pepper

To garnish

3 spring onions (scallions), chopped
4 fresh red chillies, chopped
4 shallots, chopped
60ml/4 tbsp sliced pickled mustard
    leaves, rinsed
30ml/2 tbsp fried sliced garlic
coriander (cilantro) leaves
4–6 fried noodle nests (optional)

Nowadays a signature dish of the city of Chiang Mai, this delicious noodle soup originated in Burma, now called Myanmar, which lies only a little to the north. It is also the Thai equivalent of the famous Malaysian "Laksa".

Tung Tong

Makes 18

18 wonton wrappers, about
  8cm/3¼in square, thawed
  if frozen
oil, for deep-frying
plum sauce, to serve

For the filling

4 baby corn cobs
130g/4½oz can water chestnuts,
  drained and chopped
1 shallot, coarsely chopped
1 egg, separated
30ml/2 tbsp cornflour (cornstarch)
60ml/4 tbsp water
small bunch fresh coriander
  (cilantro), chopped
salt and ground black pepper

1 Make the filling. Place the baby corn, water chestnuts, shallot and egg yolk in a food processor or blender. Process to a coarse paste. Place the egg white in a cup and whisk it lightly with a fork.

2 Put the cornflour in a small pan and stir in the water until smooth. Add the corn mixture and chopped coriander and season with salt and pepper to taste. Cook over a low heat, stirring constantly, until thickened.

3 Leave the filling to cool slightly, then place 5ml/1 tsp in the centre of a spring roll wrapper. Brush the edges with the beaten egg white, then gather up the points and press them firmly together to make a pouch or bag.

4 Repeat with remaining wrappers and filling. Heat the oil in a deep-fryer or wok to 190°C/375°F or until a cube of bread, added to the oil, browns in about 45 seconds. Fry the bags, in batches, for about 5 minutes, until golden brown. Drain on kitchen paper and serve hot, with the plum sauce.

Popularly called "gold bags", these crisp pastry purses have a coriander-flavoured filling based on water chestnuts and corn. They are the perfect vegetarian snack.

Makes 16

16 large, raw king prawns (jumbo shrimp), heads and shells removed but tails left on
5ml/1 tsp red curry paste
15ml/1 tbsp Thai fish sauce
16 small wonton wrappers, about 8cm/3¼in square, thawed if frozen
16 fine egg noodles, soaked (see Cook's Tip)
oil, for deep-frying

Firecrackers

1 Place the prawns on their sides and cut two slits through the underbelly of each, one about 1cm/½in from the head end and the other about 1cm/½in from the first cut, cutting across the prawn. This will prevent the prawns from curling when they are cooked.

2 Mix the curry paste with the fish sauce in a shallow dish. Add the prawns and turn them in the mixture until they are well coated. Cover and leave to marinate for 10 minutes.

3 Place a wonton wrapper on the work surface at an angle so that it forms a diamond shape, then fold the top corner over so that the point is in the centre. Place a prawn, slits down, on the wrapper, with the tail projecting from the folded end, then fold the bottom corner over the other end of the prawn.

4 Fold each side of the wrapper over in turn to make a tightly folded roll. Tie a noodle in a bow around the roll and set it aside. Repeat with the remaining prawns and wrappers.

5 Heat the oil in a deep-fryer or wok to 190°C/375°F or until a cube of bread, added to the oil, browns in 45 seconds. Fry the prawns, a few at a time, for 5–8 minutes, until golden brown and cooked through. Drain well on kitchen paper and keep hot while you cook the remaining batches.

COOK'S TIP
Soak the fine egg noodles used as ties for the prawn rolls in a bowl of boiling water for 2–3 minutes, until softened, then drain, refresh under cold running water and drain well again.

It's easy to see how these pastry-wrapped prawn snacks got their name (krathak in Thai) – as well as resembling fireworks, their contents explode with flavour.

Roasted Coconut Cashew Nuts

Serves 6–8

15ml/1 tbsp groundnut (peanut) oil
30ml/2 tbsp clear honey
250g/9oz/2 cups cashew nuts
115g/4oz/1⅓ cups desiccated (dry
    unsweetened shredded) coconut
2 small fresh red chillies, seeded and
    finely chopped
salt and ground black pepper

Serve these hot and sweet cashew nuts in paper or cellophane cones at parties. Not only do they look enticing and taste terrific, but the cones help to keep clothes and hands clean and can simply be thrown away afterwards.

1 Heat the oil in a wok or large frying pan and then stir in the honey. After a few seconds add the nuts and coconut and stir-fry until both are golden brown.

2 Add the chillies, with salt and pepper to taste. Toss until all the ingredients are well mixed. Serve warm or cooled in paper cones or saucers.

VARIATIONS

Whole almonds also work well, or, if you prefer, choose peanuts for a more economical snack.

Corn Fritters

Makes 12

3 corn cobs, total weight about
   250g/9oz
1 garlic clove, crushed
small bunch fresh coriander
   (cilantro), chopped
1 small fresh red or green chilli,
   seeded and finely chopped
1 spring onion (scallion), finely
   chopped
15ml/1 tbsp soy sauce
75g/3oz/¾ cup rice flour or plain
   (all-purpose) flour
2 eggs, lightly beaten
60ml/4 tbsp water
oil, for shallow frying
salt and ground black pepper
sweet chilli sauce, to serve

1 Using a sharp knife, slice the kernels from the cobs and place them in a large bowl. Add the garlic, chopped coriander, red or green chilli, spring onion, soy sauce, flour, beaten eggs and water and mix well. Season with salt and pepper to taste and mix again. The mixture should be firm enough to hold its shape, but not stiff.

2 Heat the oil in a large frying pan. Add spoonfuls of the corn mixture, gently spreading each one out with the back of the spoon to make a roundish fritter. Cook for 1–2 minutes on each side.

3 Drain on kitchen paper and keep hot while frying more fritters in the same way. Serve hot with sweet chilli sauce.

Sometimes it is the simplest dishes that taste the best. These fritters, packed with crunchy corn, are very easy to prepare and understandably popular.

Fried Egg Salad

Serves 2

15ml/1 tbsp groundnut (peanut) oil
1 garlic clove, thinly sliced
4 eggs
2 shallots, thinly sliced
2 small fresh red chillies, seeded and
  thinly sliced
½ small cucumber, finely diced
1cm/½in piece fresh root ginger,
  peeled and grated
juice of 2 limes
30ml/2 tbsp soy sauce
5ml/1 tsp caster (superfine) sugar
small bunch coriander (cilantro)
bunch watercress, coarsely chopped

1 Heat the oil in a frying pan. Add the garlic and cook over a low heat until it starts to turn golden. Crack in the eggs. Break the yolks with a wooden spatula, then fry until the eggs are almost firm. Remove from the pan and set aside.

2 Mix the shallots, chillies, cucumber and ginger in a bowl. In a separate bowl, whisk the lime juice with the soy sauce and sugar. Pour this dressing over the vegetables and toss lightly.

3 Set aside a few coriander sprigs for the garnish. Chop the rest and add them to the salad. Toss it again.

4 Reserve a few watercress sprigs and arrange the remainder on two serving plates. Cut the fried eggs into slices and divide them between the watercress mounds. Spoon the shallot mixture over them and serve, garnished with the reserved coriander and watercress.

Chillies and eggs may seem unlikely partners, but actually work very well together. The peppery flavour of the watercress makes it the perfect foundation for this tasty salad.

Hot and Sour Noodle Salad

Serves 2

200g/7oz thin rice noodles
small bunch fresh coriander (cilantro)
2 tomatoes, seeded and sliced
130g/4½oz baby corn cobs, sliced
4 spring onions (scallions), thinly
   sliced
1 red (bell) pepper, seeded and
   finely chopped
juice of 2 limes
2 small fresh green chillies, seeded
   and finely chopped
10ml/2 tsp granulated sugar
115g/4oz/1 cup peanuts, toasted
   and chopped
30ml/2 tbsp soy sauce
salt

*Noodles make the perfect
basis for a salad, absorbing
the dressing and providing a
contrast in texture to the
crisp vegetables.*

1 Bring a large pan of lightly salted water to the boil. Snap the noodles into short lengths, add to the pan and cook for 3–4 minutes. Drain, then rinse under cold water and drain again.

2 Set aside a few coriander leaves for the garnish. Chop the remaining leaves and place them in a large serving bowl.

3 Add the noodles to the bowl, with the tomato slices, corn cobs, spring onions, red pepper, lime juice, chillies, sugar and toasted peanuts. Season with the soy sauce, then taste and add a little salt if you think the mixture needs it. Toss the salad lightly but thoroughly, then garnish with the reserved coriander leaves and serve immediately.

Tofu and Green Bean Red Curry

Serves 4–6

600ml/1 pint/2½ cups canned
   coconut milk
15ml/1 tbsp Thai red curry paste
45ml/3 tbsp Thai fish sauce
10ml/2 tsp palm sugar or light
   muscovado (brown) sugar
225g/8oz/3¼ cups button
   (white) mushrooms
115g/4oz/scant 1 cup green
   beans, trimmed
175g/6oz firm tofu, rinsed, drained
   and cut in 2cm/¾in cubes
2 fresh red chillies
4 kaffir lime leaves, torn
fresh coriander (cilantro) leaves,
   to garnish

1 Pour about one-third of the coconut milk into a wok or pan. Cook until it starts to separate and an oily sheen appears on the surface.

2 Add the red curry paste, fish sauce and sugar to the coconut milk. Mix thoroughly, then add the mushrooms. Stir and cook for 1 minute.

3 Stir in the remaining coconut milk. Bring back to the boil, then add the green beans and tofu cubes. Simmer gently for 4–5 minutes more.

4 Seed the chillies and slice thinly.

5 Stir in the kaffir lime leaves and sliced red chillies. Spoon the curry into a serving dish, garnish with the coriander leaves and serve immediately.

This is one of those versatile recipes that should be in every cook's repertoire. This version uses green beans, but other types of vegetable work equally well. The tofu takes on the flavour of the spice paste and also boosts the nutritional value.

Aubergine and Pepper Tempura with Sweet Chilli Dip

1 Using a sharp knife or a mandolin, slice the aubergines into thin batons. Halve, seed and slice the red peppers thinly.

2 Make the dip. Mix together all the ingredients and stir until the sugar has dissolved. Cover with clear film (plastic wrap) and set aside.

3 Make the tempura batter. Set aside 30ml/2 tbsp of the flour. Put the egg yolks in a bowl and beat in the iced water. Tip in the remaining flour with the salt and stir together – the mixture should resemble thick pancake batter but be lumpy and not properly mixed. If it is too thick, add a little more iced water. Do not leave the batter to stand; use it immediately.

4 Pour the oil for deep-frying into a wok or deep-fryer and heat to 190°C/375°F or until a cube of bread, added to the oil, browns in about 30 seconds.

5 Pick up a small handful of aubergine batons and pepper slices, dust it with the reserved flour, then dip it into the batter. Immediately drop the batter-coated vegetables into the hot oil, taking care as the oil will froth up furiously. Repeat to make two or three more fritters, but do not cook any more than this at one time, or the oil may overflow.

6 Cook the fritters for 3–4 minutes, until they are golden and crisp all over, then lift them out with a metal basket or slotted spoon. Drain thoroughly on kitchen paper and keep hot.

7 Repeat until all the vegetables have been coated in batter and cooked. Serve immediately, with the dip.

These crunchy vegetables in a beautifully light batter are quick and easy to make and taste very good with the piquant dip.

Serves 4
2 aubergines (eggplant)
2 red (bell) peppers
vegetable oil, for deep-frying

For the tempura batter
250g/9oz/2¼ cups plain
   (all-purpose) flour
2 egg yolks
500ml/17fl oz/2¼ cups iced water
5ml/1 tsp salt

For the dip
150ml/¼ pint/⅔ cup water
10ml/2 tsp granulated sugar
1 fresh red chilli, seeded and
   finely chopped
1 garlic clove, crushed
juice of ½ lime
5ml/1 tsp rice vinegar
35ml/2½ tbsp Thai fish sauce
½ small carrot, finely grated

Serves 4

30ml/2 tbsp vegetable oil
4 garlic cloves, crushed
4 shallots, finely chopped
30ml/2 tbsp yellow curry paste
600ml/1 pint/2½ cups vegetable
  stock
2 kaffir lime leaves, torn
15ml/1 tbsp chopped fresh galangal
450g/1lb pumpkin, peeled, seeded
  and diced
225g/8oz sweet potatoes, diced
90g/3½oz/scant 1 cup peanuts,
  roasted and chopped
300ml/½ pint/1¼ cups coconut milk
90g/3½oz/1½ cups chestnut
  mushrooms, sliced
15ml/1 tbsp soy sauce
30ml/2 tbsp Thai fish sauce
50g/2oz/⅓ cup pumpkin seeds,
  toasted, and fresh green chilli
  flowers, to garnish

Sweet Pumpkin and Peanut Curry

1 Heat the oil in a large pan. Add the garlic and shallots and cook over a medium heat, stirring occasionally, for 10 minutes, until softened and golden. Do not let them burn.

2 Add the yellow curry paste and stir-fry over a medium heat for 30 seconds, until fragrant, then add the stock, lime leaves, galangal, pumpkin and sweet potatoes. Bring to the boil, stirring frequently, then reduce the heat to low and simmer gently for 15 minutes.

3 Add the peanuts, coconut milk and mushrooms. Stir in the soy sauce and fish sauce and simmer for 5 minutes more. Spoon into warmed individual serving bowls, garnish with the pumpkin seeds and chillies and serve.

COOK'S TIP

The well-drained vegetables from any of these curries would make a very tasty filling for a pastry or pie. This may not be a Thai tradition, but it is a good example of fusion food.

A hearty, soothing curry perfect for autumn or winter evenings. Its cheerful colour alone will brighten you up – and it tastes terrific.

Stir-fried Crispy Tofu

Serves 2

250g/9oz fried tofu cubes
30ml/2 tbsp groundnut (peanut) oil
15ml/1 tbsp Thai green curry paste
30ml/2 tbsp light soy sauce
2 kaffir lime leaves, rolled into
    cylinders and thinly sliced
30ml/2 tbsp granulated sugar
150ml/¼ pint/⅔ cup vegetable stock
250g/9oz Asian asparagus, trimmed
    and sliced into 5cm/2in lengths
30ml/2 tbsp roasted peanuts,
    finely chopped

The asparagus grown in Asia tends to have slender stalks. Look for it in Thai markets or substitute the thin asparagus popularly known as sprue.

1 Preheat the grill or broiler to medium. Place the tofu cubes in a grill pan and grill (broil) for 2–3 minutes, then turn them over and continue to cook until they are crisp and golden brown all over. Watch them carefully; they must not be allowed to burn.

2 Heat the oil in a wok or frying pan. Add the green curry paste and cook, stirring constantly, for 1–2 minutes, until it gives off its aroma.

3 Stir the soy sauce, lime leaves, sugar and vegetable stock into the wok or pan and mix well. Bring to the boil, then reduce the heat to low so that the mixture is just simmering.

4 Add the asparagus and simmer gently for 5 minutes. Meanwhile, chop each piece of tofu into four, then add to the pan with the peanuts.

5 Toss to coat all the ingredients in the sauce, then spoon into a warmed dish and serve immediately.

Stir-fried Seeds and Vegetables

Serves 4

30ml/2 tbsp vegetable oil
30ml/2 tbsp sesame seeds
30ml/2 tbsp sunflower seeds
30ml/2 tbsp pumpkin seeds
2 garlic cloves, finely chopped
2.5cm/1in piece fresh root ginger,
    peeled and finely chopped
2 large carrots, cut into batons
2 large courgettes (zucchini), cut
    into batons
90g/3½oz/1½ cups oyster
    mushrooms, torn in pieces
150g/5oz watercress or spinach
    leaves, coarsely chopped
small bunch fresh mint or coriander
    (cilantro), chopped
60ml/4 tbsp black bean sauce
30ml/2 tbsp light soy sauce
15ml/1 tbsp palm sugar
30ml/2 tbsp rice vinegar

*The contrast between the
crunchy seeds and
vegetables and the rich,
savoury sauce is what
makes this dish so
delicious. Serve it solo, or
with rice or noodles.*

1 Heat the oil in a wok or large frying pan. Add the seeds. Toss over a medium heat for 1 minute, then add the garlic and ginger and continue to stir-fry until the ginger is aromatic and the garlic is golden. Do not let the garlic burn or it will taste bitter.

2 Add the carrot and courgette batons and the sliced mushrooms to the wok or pan and stir-fry over a medium heat for a further 5 minutes, or until all the vegetables are crisp-tender and are golden at the edges.

3 Add the watercress or spinach with the fresh herbs. Toss over the heat for 1 minute, then stir in the black bean sauce, soy sauce, sugar and vinegar. Stir-fry for 1–2 minutes, until combined and hot. Serve immediately.

COOK'S TIP

Oyster mushrooms are delicate, so it is usually better to tear them into pieces along the lines of the gills, rather than slice them with a knife.

Chicken and Lemon Grass Curry

Serves 4

45ml/3 tbsp vegetable oil
2 garlic cloves, crushed
500g/1¼lb skinless, boneless
    chicken thighs, chopped into
    small pieces
45ml/3 tbsp Thai fish sauce
120ml/4fl oz/½ cup chicken stock
5ml/1 tsp granulated sugar
1 lemon grass stalk, chopped into
    4 sticks and lightly crushed
5 kaffir lime leaves, rolled into
    cylinders and thinly sliced across,
    plus extra to garnish
chopped roasted peanuts and
    chopped fresh coriander (cilantro),
    to garnish

For the curry paste

1 lemon grass stalk, coarsely
    chopped
2.5cm/1in piece fresh galangal,
    peeled and coarsely chopped
2 kaffir lime leaves, chopped
3 shallots, coarsely chopped
6 coriander (cilantro) roots, coarsely
    chopped
2 garlic cloves
2 fresh green chillies, seeded and
    coarsely chopped
5ml/1 tsp shrimp paste
5ml/1 tsp ground turmeric

1 Make the curry paste. Place all the ingredients in a large mortar, or food processor and pound with a pestle or process to a smooth paste.

2 Heat the vegetable oil in a wok or large, heavy frying pan, add the garlic and cook over a low heat, stirring frequently, until golden brown. Be careful not to let the garlic burn or it will taste bitter. Add the curry paste and stir-fry with the garlic for about 30 seconds more.

3 Add the chicken pieces to the pan and stir until thoroughly coated with the curry paste. Stir in the Thai fish sauce and chicken stock, with the sugar, and cook, stirring constantly, for 2 minutes more.

4 Add the lemon grass and lime leaves, reduce the heat and simmer for 10 minutes. If the mixture is dry, add a little more stock or water.

5 Remove the lemon grass, if you like. Spoon the curry into four dishes, garnish with the lime leaves, peanuts and coriander and serve.

This fragrant and truly delicious curry is exceptionally easy and takes less than twenty minutes to prepare and cook – a perfect mid-week meal.

Duck and Sesame Stir-fry

Serves 4

250g/9oz boneless wild duck meat
15ml/1 tbsp sesame oil
15ml/1 tbsp vegetable oil
4 garlic cloves, finely sliced
2.5ml/½ tsp dried chilli flakes
15ml/1 tbsp Thai fish sauce
15ml/1 tbsp light soy sauce
120ml/4fl oz/½ cup water
1 head broccoli, cut into small florets
coriander (cilantro) and 15ml/1 tbsp
   toasted sesame seeds, to garnish

1 Cut the duck meat into bitesize pieces. Heat the oils in a wok or large, heavy frying pan and stir-fry the garlic over a medium heat until it is golden brown – do not let it burn.

2 Add the duck to the pan and stir-fry for a further 2 minutes, until the meat begins to brown.

3 Stir in the chilli flakes, fish sauce, soy sauce and water. Add the broccoli and continue to stir-fry for about 2 minutes, until the duck is just cooked through.

4 Serve on warmed plates, garnished with coriander and sesame seeds.

VARIATIONS

Pak choi (bok choy) or Chinese flowering cabbage can be used instead of broccoli.

This recipe comes from northern Thailand and is intended for game birds, as farmed duck would have too much fat. Use wild duck if you can get it, or even partridge, pheasant or pigeon. If you do use farmed duck, you should remove the skin and fat layer.

Stir-fried Beef in Oyster Sauce

1 Place the steak in the freezer for 30–40 minutes, until firm, then, using a sharp knife, slice it on the diagonal into long thin strips.

2 Mix together the soy sauce and cornflour in a large bowl. Add the steak, turning to coat well, cover with clear film (plastic wrap) and leave to marinate at room temperature for 1–2 hours.

3 Heat half the oil in a wok or large, heavy frying pan. Add the garlic and ginger and cook for 1–2 minutes, until fragrant. Drain the steak, add it to the wok or pan and stir well to separate the strips. Cook, stirring frequently, for a further 1–2 minutes, until the steak is browned all over and tender. Remove from the wok or pan and set aside.

4 Heat the remaining oil in the wok or pan. Add the shiitake, oyster and straw mushrooms. Stir-fry over a medium heat until golden brown.

5 Return the steak to the wok and mix it with the mushrooms. Spoon in the oyster sauce and sugar, mix well, then add ground black pepper to taste. Toss over the heat until all the ingredients are thoroughly combined.

6 Stir in the spring onions. Tip the mixture on to a serving platter, garnish with the strips of red chilli and serve.

Serves 4–6

450g/1lb rump (round) steak
30ml/2 tbsp soy sauce
15ml/1 tbsp cornflour (cornstarch)
45ml/3 tbsp vegetable oil
15ml/1 tbsp chopped garlic
15ml/1 tbsp chopped fresh root
  ginger
225g/8oz/3¼ cups mixed
  mushrooms such as shiitake,
  oyster and straw
30ml/2 tbsp oyster sauce
5ml/1 tsp granulated sugar
4 spring onions (scallions), cut into
  short lengths
ground black pepper
2 fresh red chillies, seeded and cut
  into strips, to garnish

Another simple but delicious recipe. In Thailand this is often made with just straw mushrooms, which are readily available fresh, but oyster mushrooms make a good substitute and using a mixture makes the dish extra interesting.

Serves 4–6

450g/1lb beef sirloin
15ml/1 tbsp vegetable oil
45ml/3 tbsp Thai green curry paste
600ml/1 pint/2½ cups coconut milk
4 kaffir lime leaves, torn
15–30ml/1–2 tbsp Thai fish sauce
5ml/1 tsp palm sugar or light
   muscovado (brown) sugar
150g/5oz small Thai aubergines
   (eggplant), halved
a small handful of fresh Thai basil
2 fresh green chillies, to garnish

Green Beef Curry with Thai Aubergines

1 Trim off any excess fat from the beef. Using a sharp knife, cut it into long, thin strips. This is easiest to do if it is well chilled. Set it aside.

2 Heat the oil in a large, heavy pan or wok. Add the curry paste and cook for 1–2 minutes, until it is fragrant.

3 Stir in half the coconut milk, a little at a time. Cook, stirring frequently, for approximately 5–6 minutes, until an oily sheen appears on the surface of the liquid.

4 Add the beef to the pan with the kaffir lime leaves, Thai fish sauce, sugar and aubergine halves. Cook for 2–3 minutes, then stir in the remaining coconut milk.

5 Bring back to a simmer and cook until the meat and aubergines are tender. Stir in the Thai basil just before serving. Finely shred the green chillies and use to garnish the curry.

COOK'S TIP

To make the green curry paste, put 15 fresh green chillies, 2 chopped lemon grass stalks, 3 sliced shallots, 2 garlic cloves, 15ml/1 tbsp chopped galangal, 4 chopped kaffir lime leaves, 2.5ml/½ tsp grated kaffir lime rind, 5ml/1 tsp chopped coriander root, 6 black peppercorns, 5ml/1 tsp each roasted coriander and cumin seeds, 15ml/1 tbsp granulated sugar, 5ml/1 tsp salt and 5ml/1 tsp shrimp paste into a food processor and process until smooth. Gradually add 30ml/2 tbsp vegetable oil, processing after each addition.

This is a very quick curry so be sure to use good quality meat. Sirloin is recommended, but tender rump (round) steak could be used instead

Sweet and Sour Pork, Thai-style

Serves 4

350g/12oz lean pork
30ml/2 tbsp vegetable oil
4 garlic cloves, thinly sliced
1 small red onion, sliced
30ml/2 tbsp Thai fish sauce
15ml/1 tbsp granulated sugar
1 red (bell) pepper, seeded and diced
½ cucumber, seeded and sliced
2 plum tomatoes, cut into wedges
115g/4oz piece of fresh pineapple,
    cut into small chunks
2 spring onions (scallions), cut into
    short lengths
ground black pepper
coriander (cilantro) leaves and
    spring onions (scallions),
    shredded, to garnish

*It was the Chinese who
originally created sweet and
sour cooking, but the Thais
also do it very well. This
version has a fresher and
cleaner flavour than the
original. It makes a good
one-dish meal when
served over rice.*

1 Place the pork in the freezer for 30–40 minutes, until firm. Using a sharp knife, cut it into thin strips.

2 Heat the oil in a wok or large frying pan. Add the garlic. Cook over a medium heat until golden, then add the pork and stir-fry for 4–5 minutes. Add the onion slices and toss to mix.

3 Add the fish sauce, sugar and ground black pepper to taste. Toss the mixture over the heat for 3–4 minutes more.

4 Stir in the red pepper, cucumber, tomatoes, pineapple and spring onions. Stir-fry for 3–4 minutes more, then spoon into a bowl. Garnish with the coriander and spring onions and serve.

Pork Belly with Five Spices

Serves 4

1 large bunch fresh coriander
   (cilantro) with roots
30ml/2 tbsp vegetable oil
1 garlic clove, crushed
30ml/2 tbsp five-spice powder
500g/1¼lb pork belly, cut into
   2.5cm/1in pieces
400g/14oz can chopped tomatoes
150ml/¼ pint/⅔ cup hot water
30ml/2 tbsp dark soy sauce
45ml/3 tbsp Thai fish sauce
30ml/2 tbsp granulated sugar
boiled rice, to serve

*The Chinese influence on
Thai cuisine stems from the
early years of its history,
when colonists from
southern China settled in
the country, bringing with
them dishes like this,
although Thai cooks
have provided their own
unique imprint.*

1 Cut off the coriander roots. Chop five of them finely and freeze the remainder for another occasion. Chop the coriander stalks and leaves and set them aside. Keep the roots separate.

2 Heat the oil in a large pan and cook the garlic until golden brown. Stirring constantly, add the chopped coriander roots and then the five-spice powder.

3 Add the pork and stir-fry until the meat is thoroughly coated in spices and has browned. Stir in the tomatoes and hot water. Bring to the boil, then stir in the soy sauce, fish sauce and sugar.

4 Reduce the heat, cover the pan and simmer for 30 minutes. Stir in the chopped coriander stalks and leaves, squeeze over the lime juice and serve with rice.

Northern Fish Curry with Shallots and Lemon Grass

Serves 4

450g/1lb salmon fillet
500ml/17fl oz/2¼ cups vegetable
    stock
4 shallots, finely chopped
2 garlic cloves, finely chopped
2.5cm/1in piece fresh galangal, finely
    chopped
1 lemon grass stalk, finely chopped
2.5ml/½ tsp dried chilli flakes
15ml/1 tbsp Thai fish sauce
5ml/1 tsp palm sugar or light
    muscovado (brown) sugar

1 Place the salmon in the freezer for 30–40 minutes to firm up the flesh slightly. Remove and discard the skin, then use a sharp knife to cut the fish into 2.5cm/1in cubes, removing any stray bones with your fingers or with tweezers as you do so.

2 Pour the stock into a large, heavy pan and bring it to the boil over a medium heat. Add the shallots, garlic, galangal, lemon grass, chilli flakes, fish sauce and sugar. Bring back to the boil, stir well, then reduce the heat and simmer gently for 15 minutes.

3 Add the fish, bring back to the boil, then turn off the heat. Leave the curry to stand for 10–15 minutes until the fish is cooked through, then serve.

COOK'S TIP

Fresh lemon grass is available in Asian stores and supermarkets. To prepare, peel away and discard the fibrous layers surrounding the stalk. Only the bottom 10–15cm/4–6in end of the stalk is used in recipes.

This is a thin, soupy curry with wonderfully strong flavours. Serve it in bowls with lots of sticky rice to soak up the delicious juices.

Stir-fried Squid with Ginger

Serves 2

4 ready-prepared baby squid, total
    weight about 250g/9oz
15ml/1 tbsp vegetable oil
2 garlic cloves, finely chopped
30ml/2 tbsp soy sauce
2.5cm/1in piece fresh root ginger,
    peeled and finely chopped
juice of ½ lemon
5ml/1 tsp granulated sugar
2 spring onions (scallions), chopped

1 Rinse the squid well and pat dry with kitchen paper. Cut the bodies into rings and halve the tentacles, if necessary.

2 Heat the oil in a wok or frying pan and cook the garlic until golden brown, but do not let it burn. Add the squid and stir-fry for 30 seconds over a high heat.

3 Add the soy sauce, ginger, lemon juice, sugar and spring onions. Stir-fry a further 30 seconds, then serve.

COOK'S TIP

Squid has an undeserved reputation for being rubbery in texture. This is always a result of overcooking it.

The abundance of fish around the Gulf of Thailand sustains thriving markets for the restaurant and hotel trade, and every market naturally features stalls where delicious, freshly-caught seafood is cooked and served. This recipe is very popular among street traders.

Hot and Fragrant Trout

Serves 4

2 large fresh green chillies, seeded
and coarsely chopped
5 shallots, peeled
5 garlic cloves, peeled
30ml/2 tbsp fresh lime juice
30ml/2 tbsp Thai fish sauce
15ml/1 tbsp palm sugar or light
muscovado (brown) sugar
4 kaffir lime leaves, rolled into
cylinders and thinly sliced
2 trout or similar firm-fleshed fish,
about 350g/12oz each, cleaned
fresh garlic chives, to garnish
boiled rice, to serve

*This wickedly hot spice
paste could be used as a
marinade for any fish or
meat. It also makes a
wonderful spicy dip for
grilled meat.*

1 Wrap the chillies, shallots and garlic in a foil package. Place under a
hot grill or broiler for 10 minutes, until softened.

2 When the package is cool enough to handle, tip the contents into a
mortar or food processor and pound with a pestle or process to a paste.

3 Add the lime juice, fish sauce, sugar and lime leaves and mix well.
With a teaspoon, stuff this paste inside the fish. Smear a little on the
skin too. Grill (broil) the fish for about 5 minutes on each side, until just
cooked through. Lift the fish on to a platter, garnish with garlic chives
and serve with rice.

Festive Rice

Serves 8

450g/1lb/2⅔ cups jasmine rice
60ml/4 tbsp oil
2 garlic cloves, crushed
2 onions, thinly sliced
2.5ml/½ tsp ground turmeric
750ml/1¼ pints/3 cups water
400ml/14fl oz can coconut milk
1–2 lemon grass stalks, bruised

For the accompaniments

omelette strips (see page 18)
2 fresh red chillies, seeded
    and shredded
cucumber chunks
tomato wedges
deep-fried onions
prawn (shrimp) crackers

1 Put the jasmine rice in a large strainer and rinse it thoroughly under cold water. Drain well.

2 Heat the oil in a frying pan with a lid. Cook the garlic, onions and turmeric over a low heat for 2–3 minutes, until the onions have softened. Add the rice and stir well to coat in oil.

3 Pour in the water and coconut milk and add the lemon grass. Bring to the boil, stirring. Cover the pan and cook gently for 12 minutes, or until all the liquid has been absorbed by the rice.

4 Remove the pan from the heat and lift the lid. Cover with a clean dishtowel, replace the lid and leave to stand in a warm place for 15 minutes. Remove the lemon grass, mound the rice mixture in a cone on a serving platter and garnish with the accompaniments, then serve.

COOK'S TIP

Jasmine rice is widely available in most supermarkets and Asian stores. It is also known as Thai fragrant rice.

This pretty Thai dish is traditionally shaped into a cone and surrounded by a variety of accompaniments before being served.

Rice Cakes with a Prawn and Coconut Dip

1 Rinse the rice in a sieve under running cold water until the water runs clear, then place the rice in a large, heavy pan and pour over the measured boiling water. Stir, bring back to the boil, then reduce the heat and simmer, uncovered, for 15 minutes, by which time almost all the water should have been absorbed or evaporated.

Serves 4–6

150g/5oz/scant 1 cup jasmine rice
400ml/14fl oz/1⅔ cups boiling water

2 Reduce the heat to the lowest possible setting – use a heat diffuser if you have one. Cook the rice for a further 2 hours, by which time it should be crisp and stuck to the base of the pan. Continue to cook for a further 5–10 minutes, until the sides of the rice cake begin to come away from the edges of the pan.

For the dip

1 garlic clove, coarsely chopped
small bunch fresh coriander
    (cilantro), coarsely chopped
90g/3½oz cooked prawns (shrimp),
    peeled and deveined
250ml/8fl oz/1 cup coconut milk
15ml/1 tbsp Thai fish sauce
15ml/1 tbsp light soy sauce
15ml/1 tbsp tamarind juice, made by
    mixing tamarind pulp with warm
    water
5ml/1 tsp palm sugar or light
    muscovado (brown) sugar
30ml/2 tbsp roasted peanuts,
    coarsely chopped
1 fresh red chilli, seeded and
    chopped

3 Preheat the oven to 180°C/350°F/Gas 4. Remove the rice cake by gently easing the tip of a knife under the edges to loosen it all around. Place it on a baking sheet. Bake the rice cake for 20 minutes, until it is golden and crisp, then leave it to cool.

4 Meanwhile, make the dip. Place all the ingredients in a food processor and process to a smooth paste. Tip into a wide serving bowl. Serve the rice cake with the dip. It can either be left whole for guests to break, or sliced or broken into pieces by the cook.

VARIATION
If you don't have time to make your own rice cakes, you could use the ones sold in packets in supermarkets. The texture of the bought product is very different and the flavour bland, but it will be improved by the dip.

These wonderfully crunchy rice cakes take some time to prepare but are very easy to make. The dip is delicious and goes well with other dishes; try it with balls of sticky rice.

Chiang Mai Noodles

1 Pour the coconut cream into a large wok or frying pan and bring to the boil over a medium heat. Continue to boil, stirring frequently, for 8–10 minutes, until the milk separates and an oily sheen appears on the surface.

2 Add the magic paste and red curry paste and cook, stirring constantly, for 3–5 seconds, until fragrant.

3 Add the chicken and toss over the heat until sealed on all sides. Stir in the soy sauce and the diced peppers and stir-fry for 3–4 minutes. Pour in the stock. Bring to the boil, then lower the heat and simmer for 10–15 minutes, until the chicken is fully cooked.

4 Meanwhile, make the noodle garnish. Heat the oil in a pan or deep-fryer to 190°C/375°F or until a cube of bread, added to the oil, browns in 45 seconds. Break all the noodles in half, then divide them into four portions. Add one portion at a time to the hot oil. They will puff up on contact. As soon as they are crisp, lift the noodles out with a slotted spoon and drain on kitchen paper.

5 Bring a large pan of water to the boil and cook the noodles until tender, following the instructions on the packet. Drain well, divide among four warmed dishes, then spoon the curry sauce over them. Top each portion with a cluster of fried noodles. Sprinkle the chopped pickled garlic and coriander over the top and serve immediately, with lime wedges.

COOK'S TIP
Thai magic paste is a vibrant mixture of fresh coriander (cilantro), garlic, white pepper and fish source. It is available as a ready-made paste.

An interesting noodle dish that combines soft, boiled noodles with crisp deep-fried ones and adds the usual panoply of Thai sweet, hot and sour flavours.

Serves 4
250ml/8fl oz/1 cup coconut cream
15ml/1 tbsp magic paste
5ml/1 tsp Thai red curry paste
450g/1lb chicken thigh meat,
    chopped into small pieces
30ml/2 tbsp dark soy sauce
2 red (bell) peppers, seeded and
    finely diced
600ml/1 pint/2½ cups chicken or
    vegetable stock
90g/3½oz fresh or dried rice noodles

For the garnishes
vegetable oil, for deep-frying
90g/3½oz fine dried rice noodles
2 pickled garlic cloves, chopped
small bunch fresh coriander
    (cilantro), chopped
2 limes, cut into wedges

Mee Krob

Serves 1

vegetable oil, for deep-frying
130g/4½oz rice vermicelli noodles

For the sauce

30ml/2 tbsp vegetable oil
130g/4½oz fried tofu, cut into
    thin strips
2 garlic cloves, finely chopped
2 small shallots, finely chopped
15ml/1 tbsp light soy sauce
30ml/2 tbsp palm sugar or light
    muscovado (brown) sugar
60ml/4 tbsp vegetable stock
juice of 1 lime
2.5ml/½ tsp dried chilli flakes

For the garnish

15ml/1 tbsp vegetable oil
1 egg, lightly beaten with 15ml/1
    tbsp cold water
25g/1oz/⅓ cup beansprouts
1 spring onion (scallion), thinly
    shredded
1 fresh red chilli, seeded and
    finely chopped
1 whole head pickled garlic, sliced
    across the bulb so each slice looks
    like a flower

1 Heat the oil for deep-frying in a wok or large pan to 190°C/375°F or until a cube of bread, added to the oil, browns in about 45 seconds. Add the noodles and deep-fry until golden and crisp. Drain on kitchen paper and set aside.

2 Make the sauce. Heat the oil in a wok, add the fried tofu and cook over a medium heat until crisp. Using a slotted spoon, transfer it to a warm plate.

3 Add the garlic and shallots to the wok and cook until golden brown. Stir in the soy sauce, sugar, stock, lime juice and chilli flakes. Cook, stirring, until the mixture begins to caramelize.

4 Add the reserved tofu and stir until it has soaked up some of the liquid. Remove the wok from the heat and set aside.

5 Prepare the egg garnish. Heat the oil in a wok or frying pan. Pour in the egg in a thin stream to form trails. As soon as it sets, lift it out with a fish slice or metal spatula and place on a plate.

6 Crumble the noodles into the tofu sauce, mix well, then spoon into warmed serving bowls. Sprinkle with the beansprouts, spring onion, fried egg strips, chilli and pickled garlic "flowers" and serve immediately.

The name of this dish means "deep-fried noodles" and it is very popular in Thailand. The taste is a stunning combination of sweet and hot, salty and sour, while the texture contrives to be both crisp and chewy. To some Western palates, it may seem rather unusual, but this delicious dish is well worth making.

Watermelon Ice

Serves 4–6

90ml/6 tbsp caster (superfine) sugar

105ml/7 tbsp water

4 kaffir lime leaves, torn into small pieces

500g/1¼lb watermelon, cut into wedges, seeds removed and then chopped into 2.5cm/1in pieces.

After a hot and spicy Thai meal, the only thing more refreshing than eating ice-cold watermelon is this watermelon ice. Making it is simplicity itself.

1 Put the sugar, water and lime leaves in a pan. Heat gently until the sugar has dissolved. Pour into a large bowl and set aside to cool.

2 Spoon the watermelon into a food processor. Process to a slush, then mix thoroughly with the sugar syrup. Chill the mixture in the refrigerator for 3–4 hours.

3 Strain the mixture into a freezerproof container. Freeze for 2 hours, then remove from the freezer and beat with a fork to break up the ice crystals. Return the mixture to the freezer and freeze for 3 hours more, beating the mixture at half-hourly intervals. Freeze until firm.

4 Alternatively, use an ice cream maker. Pour the chilled mixture into the machine and churn until it is firm enough to scoop. Serve immediately, or scrape into a freezerproof container and store in the freezer.

5 About 30 minutes before serving, transfer the ice to the refrigerator so that it softens slightly. This allows the full flavour of the watermelon to be enjoyed and makes it easier to scoop.

Fried Bananas

Serves 4

115g/4oz/1 cup plain (all-
    purpose) flour
2.5ml/½ tsp bicarbonate of soda
    (baking soda)
pinch of salt
30ml/2 tbsp granulated sugar
1 egg, beaten
90ml/6 tbsp water
30ml/2 tbsp shredded coconut or
    15ml/1 tbsp sesame seeds
4 firm bananas
vegetable oil, for deep-frying
30ml/2 tbsp clear honey, to
    serve (optional)

1 Sift the flour, bicarbonate of soda and salt into a large bowl. Stir in the granulated sugar and the egg, and whisk in just enough of the water to make quite a thin batter.

2 Whisk the shredded coconut or sesame seeds into the batter.

3 Peel the bananas. Cut each one in half lengthways, then in half crossways to make 16 pieces of the same size. Don't do this until you are ready to cook them because, once peeled, bananas quickly discolour.

4 Heat the oil in a wok or deep-fryer to a temperature of 190°C/375°F or until a cube of bread, dropped in the oil, browns in about 45 seconds. Dip the banana pieces in the batter, then gently drop a few into the oil. Deep-fry until golden brown, then lift out and drain well on kitchen paper.

5 Cook the remaining banana pieces in the same way. Serve immediately with honey, if using.

These deliciously sweet treats are a favourite with children and adults alike. In Thailand, you will find them on sale from portable roadside stalls and markets at almost every hour of the day and night.

Thai-fried Pineapple

Serves 4

1 pineapple
40g/1½oz/3 tbsp butter
15ml/1 tbsp desiccated (dry
    unsweetened shredded) coconut
60ml/4 tbsp soft light brown sugar
60ml/4 tbsp fresh lime juice
lime slices, to decorate
thick and creamy natural (plain)
    yogurt, to serve

1 Using a sharp knife, cut the top off the pineapple and peel off the skin, taking care to remove the eyes. Cut the pineapple in half and remove and discard the woody core. Cut the flesh lengthways into 1cm/½in wedges.

2 Heat the butter in a large, heavy frying pan or wok. When it has melted, add the pineapple wedges and cook over a medium heat for 1–2 minutes on each side, or until they have turned pale golden in colour.

3 Meanwhile, dry-fry the coconut in a small frying pan until lightly browned. Remove from the heat and set aside.

4 Sprinkle the sugar into the pan with the pineapple, add the lime juice and cook, stirring constantly, until the sugar has dissolved. Divide the pineapple wedges among four bowls, sprinkle with the coconut, decorate with the lime slices and serve with the yogurt.

A very simple and quick Thai dessert – pineapple fried in butter, brown sugar and lime juice, and sprinkled with toasted coconut. The slightly sharp taste of the fruit makes this a very refreshing treat at the end of a meal.

Nutritional notes

Omelette Soup: Energy 68kcal/283kJ; Protein 2.7g; Carbohydrate 3.9g, of which sugars 3.6g; Fat 4.7g, of which saturates 1g; Cholesterol 55mg; Calcium 28mg; Fibre 1.1g; Sodium 772mg.

Vegetable and Tofu Soup: Energy 103kcal/434kJ; Protein 5.5g; Carbohydrate 13.3g, of which sugars 12.8g; Fat 3.5g, of which saturates 0.4g; Cholesterol 0mg; Calcium 320mg; Fibre 0.7g; Sodium 769mg.

Chiang Mai Noodle Soup: Energy 606kcal/2569kJ; Protein 39.5g; Carbohydrate 88.7g, of which sugars 10.1g; Fat 12.9g, of which saturates 3.7g; Cholesterol 135mg; Calcium 84mg; Fibre 3.3g; Sodium 1111mg.

Tung Tong: Energy 55kcal/229kJ; Protein 1.2g; Carbohydrate 6.3g, of which sugars 0.4g; Fat 2.9g, of which saturates 0.4g; Cholesterol 12mg; Calcium 19mg; Fibre 0.5g; Sodium 42mg.

Firecrackers: Energy 71kcal/298kJ; Protein 3.2g; Carbohydrate 7.1g, of which sugars 0.2g; Fat 3.5g, of which saturates 0.5g; Cholesterol 25mg; Calcium 20mg; Fibre 0.3g; Sodium 30mg.

Roasted Coconut Cashew Nuts: Energy 436kcal/1810kJ; Protein 9.7g; Carbohydrate 22.1g, of which sugars 16.6g; Fat 34.9g, of which saturates 14.8g; Cholesterol 0mg; Calcium 20mg; Fibre 4g; Sodium 128mg.

Corn Fritters: Energy 77kcal/322kJ; Protein 2.3g; Carbohydrate 7.8g, of which sugars 0.6g; Fat 4.1g, of which saturates 0.6g; Cholesterol 32mg; Calcium 24mg; Fibre 0.8g; Sodium 104mg.

Fried Egg Salad: Energy 235kcal/977kJ; Protein 14.8g; Carbohydrate 6.4g, of which sugars 5.6g; Fat 17.2g, of which saturates 3.9g; Cholesterol 381mg; Calcium 154mg; Fibre 1.2g; Sodium 1234mg

Hot and Sour Noodle Salad: Energy 761kcal/3173kJ; Protein 24.1g; Carbohydrate 101.6g, of which sugars 15.6g; Fat 27.7g, of which saturates 5.2g; Cholesterol 0mg; Calcium 117mg; Fibre 7.9g; Sodium 1840mg.

Tofu and Green Bean Red Curry: Energy 79kcal/333kJ; Protein 3.9g; Carbohydrate 8.2g, of which sugars 7.8g; Fat 3.6g, of which saturates 0.6g; Cholesterol 0mg; Calcium 189mg; Fibre 0.8g; Sodium 647mg.

Aubergine and Pepper Tempura: Energy 442kcal/1856kJ; Protein 9.5g; Carbohydrate 57.7g, of which sugars 9.6g; Fat 20.9g, of which saturates 3.1g; Cholesterol 101mg; Calcium 122mg; Fibre 6.2g; Sodium 859mg.

Sweet Pumpkin and Peanut Curry: Energy 292kcal/1218kJ; Protein 8.4g; Carbohydrate 22.2g, of which sugars 11.2g; Fat 19.5g, of which saturates 3.3g; Cholesterol 0mg; Calcium 87mg; Fibre 4.3g; Sodium 768mg.

Stir-fried Crispy Tofu: Energy 510kcal/2122kJ; Protein 33.5g; Carbohydrate 18.8g, of which sugars 17.2g; Fat 33.9g, of which saturates 2.2g; Cholesterol 0mg; Calcium 1893mg; Fibre 2.2g; Sodium 1085mg.

Stir-fried Seeds and Vegetables: Energy 205kcal/849kJ; Protein 6.9g; Carbohydrate 9.7g, of which sugars 7.7g; Fat 15.6g, of which saturates 2g; Cholesterol 0mg; Calcium 159mg; Fibre 3.4g; Sodium 294mg.

Chicken and Lemon Grass Curry: Energy 212kcal/890kJ; Protein 30.1g; Carbohydrate 1.4g, of which sugars 1.3g; Fat 9.6g, of which saturates 1.4g; Cholesterol 88mg; Calcium 8mg; Fibre 0g; Sodium 342mg.

Duck and Sesame Stir-fry: Energy 192kcal/798kJ; Protein 18.7g; Carbohydrate 2.7g, of which sugars 2.3g; Fat 12.9g, of which saturates 2.1g; Cholesterol 69mg; Calcium 104mg; Fibre 3.6g; Sodium 436mg.

Stir-fried Beef in Oyster Sauce: Energy 282kcal/1177kJ; Protein 25.4g; Carbohydrate 10.7g, of which sugars 3.4g; Fat 15.5g, of which saturates 4.2g; Cholesterol 69mg; Calcium 16mg; Fibre 0.8g; Sodium 697mg.

Green Beef Curry: Energy 226kcal/949kJ; Protein 24.7g; Carbohydrate 9.4g, of which sugars 9.3g; Fat 10.2g, of which saturates 3.8g; Cholesterol 69mg; Calcium 53mg; Fibre 0.8g; Sodium 393mg.

Sweet and Sour Pork: Energy 214kcal/894kJ; Protein 20.3g; Carbohydrate 12.5g, of which sugars 11.9g; Fat 9.5g, of which saturates 2g; Cholesterol 55mg; Calcium 34mg; Fibre 2g; Sodium 337mg.

Northern Fish Curry: Energy 212kcal/882kJ; Protein 23.1g; Carbohydrate 1.7g, of which sugars 1.6g; Fat 12.5g, of which saturates 2.2g; Cholesterol 56mg; Calcium 28mg; Fibre 0.2g; Sodium 267mg.

Stir-fried Squid with Ginger: Energy 168kcal/704kJ; Protein 19.9g; Carbohydrate 5.1g, of which sugars 3.5g; Fat 7.7g, of which saturates 1.2g; Cholesterol 281mg; Calcium 24mg; Fibre 0.2g; Sodium 1207mg.

Festive Rice: Energy 303kcal/1263kJ; Protein 6.4g; Carbohydrate 49.5g, of which sugars 4.2g; Fat 8.6g, of which saturates 2g; Cholesterol 53mg; Calcium 41mg; Fibre 0.5g; Sodium 212mg.

Rice Cakes with Dip: Energy 361kcal/1508kJ; Protein 11.7g; Carbohydrate 42g, of which sugars 8.8g; Fat 16g, of which saturates 2.9g; Cholesterol 19mg; Calcium 38mg; Fibre 0.8g; Sodium 359mg.

Chiang Mai Noodles: Energy 245kcal/1034kJ; Protein 29.4g; Carbohydrate 27.6g, of which sugars 9g; Fat 1.8g, of which saturates 0.6g; Cholesterol 79mg; Calcium 35mg; Fibre 1.4g; Sodium 677mg.

Mee Krob: Energy 995kcal/4151kJ; Protein 20.4g; Carbohydrate 140.4g, of which sugars 36.6g; Fat 39.9g, of which saturates 5.6g; Cholesterol 209mg; Calcium 102mg; Fibre 1.4g; Sodium 1161mg.

Watermelon Ice: Energy 85kcal/363kJ; Protein 0.5g; Carbohydrate 21.6g, of which sugars 21.6g; Fat 0.3g, of which saturates 0.1g; Cholesterol 0mg; Calcium 14mg; Fibre 0.1g; Sodium 3mg.

Fried Bananas: Energy 233kcal/977kJ; Protein 3g; Carbohydrate 34g, of which sugars 17g; Fat 10g, of which saturates 1g; Cholesterol 0mg; Calcium 26mg; Fibre 3g; Sodium 124mg.

Thai-fried Pineapple: Energy 115kcal/490kJ; Protein 1.2g; Carbohydrate 22g, of which sugars 21.6g; Fat 3.2g, of which saturates 0.3g; Cholesterol 0mg; Calcium 41mg; Fibre 2.6g; Sodium 539mg.

Index